Joe Biden

A Biography of an American President

Joseph Greene

Table of Contents

Introduction

Joe Biden has been a well-known political figure for decades. When he won his first bid for the senate, at only age 29, he became the fifth-youngest senator in U.S. history. He was re-elected six times, becoming the state's longest-serving senator; he represented Delaware in the senate from 1972 until 2009.

On January 20, 2021, Joseph Robinette Biden Jr., was sworn in as the 46th president of the United States. The inauguration ceremony was unique for several reasons. At 78 years old, Joseph Biden was the oldest man ever elected as president. His oath of office occurred during a much smaller and, perhaps more fortified, event than usual. This was due to both the coronavirus pandemic and the attack on the U.S. Capitol that had occurred just two weeks prior. Biden's vice president, Kamala Harris, also made history on inauguration day. The daughter of a Jamaican father and an Indian mother—both of whom moved to the United States to further their educations—became the first Black person, the first person of South Asian descent, and the first female to hold the position of vice president,

During his years in the Senate, Biden gained a reputation for his stance on tougher crime laws, especially during the eighties and nineties, and as an expert on foreign policy matters. While Biden's professional life has been one characterized by service, there have been public gaffes along the way, along with rumors of inappropriate behavior towards women.

His personal life has been rife with trauma and loss. Biden's first wife and their infant daughter were killed in a car accident in 1972; their two young sons were also seriously injured. Biden did not attend the swearing-in ceremony for new senators in Washington, choosing to take the oath of office in his son's hospital room.

As we delve deeper into these, and other, aspects of the life of the 46th president of the United States, you will gain a deeper understanding of 'Joe'—as an individual, as a family man and as a politician.

What Makes This Book Unique?

A great deal has been written about Joe Biden; a quick internet search will confirm this. This is not surprising, considering the length of time he has spent as a high-profile public figure. However, most of what has been written is politically slanted and intended to either flaunt Biden's positive attributes or accentuate the negative ones.

In this book, however, we attempt to take an objective approach to the man, his family dynamics, and his career. Generally speaking, we will be as objective as possible—and stick to the facts—while not ignoring the more controversial aspects of his life.

Unlike the literature published by his supporters, we will not focus, solely, on Biden's strengths and successes. Nor will we focus, entirely, on his flaws and shortcomings, as Biden's critics have done. This book does not seek to create a positive or a negative image of Biden but to present a balanced, objective perspective of him.

Chapter 1: The Formative Years

In this chapter, we will examine the early years of Joe's life—beginning with his family's circumstances at the time of his birth. We will look at the value system that he developed, the influential individuals in his life, and the significant events that shaped his character.

Early Years

In the midst of World War II, Joseph Robinette Biden Jr. was born on November 20, 1942, at St. Mary's Hospital in Scranton—located in northeastern Pennsylvania. Joe was the eldest child of Joseph Robinette Biden Sr. and Catherine Eugenia ('Jean') Finnegan Biden. In time, Joe Jr. was joined by a sister, Valerie, as well as two brothers James and Frank.

During the war, Biden Sr. was able to provide a financially comfortable life for his family. He worked in an executive position at his uncle's manufacturing company which provided sealant for U.S. merchant marine ships; for a time, Biden Sr. worked in the Boston office. Following the war, the family struggled financially as Biden Sr. found it difficult to find gainful employment. The family returned to Scranton, and Biden Sr. worked at a variety of odd jobs, to support his family. The situation improved in the early 1950s when he became a used car salesman.

From a young age, Biden's parents encouraged him to be resilient and to stand up for himself. According to Biden, his father often told him that, "the measure of a man is not how often he is knocked down, but how quickly he gets up". His mother also pushed the boy to be assertive. When he would come home upset about being bullied by a bigger boy, she would tell him, "Bloody their nose so you can walk down the street the next day".

Stuttering

As a boy, Biden had a severe stuttering issue which had a significant impact on his childhood and development. In a 2008 speech, he stated, "I can think of nothing else that has ever stripped me of my dignity as quickly and as profoundly and as thoroughly as when I stuttered in grade school". His debilitating stutter resulted in derogatory nicknames during high school. They included 'Joe Impedimenta' and 'Dash'—the latter, "not because he was speedy but because his schoolmates thought it sounded like Morse code when he stammered".

Biden worked hard to overcome his stuttering. With the exception of a few sessions with a speech-language pathologist during kindergarten—which Biden did not find helpful—he did not receive professional help for his stutter. However, as a young teen, he decided to work on it independently. He would stand in front of his bedroom mirror and recite poetry while holding a flashlight to his face.

Fortunately, Biden's parents were understanding and supportive. According to Biden's sister, their mother would tell him things like he was so smart that he couldn't get the words out fast enough. When Biden was humiliated in seventh grade by a nun who made fun of his stuttering, he left the classroom and walked home. Upon discovering what had happened, Biden's mother returned to the school with Biden and told the nun, "You do that again, I'll knock your bonnet off your head".

Biden seemingly had great respect for his parents, but this was not the case for his feelings toward the extended Biden and Finnegan families. While on the campaign trail in 2008, when asked why he did not drink, Biden responded, "There are enough alcoholics in my family". While there is no indication that either of Biden's parents was a heavy drinker, one of Biden's uncles–who resided with the Biden family for a time–drank heavily.

Schooling

Until the family moved to Delaware when Biden Jr. was 10 years old, he attended St. Paul's Elementary School in Scranton. Upon moving to Delaware, he initially attended St. Helena School until he was accepted at Archmere Academy, a private Catholic school. Biden had long wanted to attend school there. While his dream became a reality, Biden worked at odd jobs on the campus, including weeding the school gardens and washing windows, to offset tuition costs.

While attending Archmere, Biden was a solid academic student. He appears to have been a natural leader and was class president during both his junior and senior years. However, much to Biden's disappointment, due to the number of demerits he had received, school administration prevented him from running for student body president.

He was also a natural athlete, excelling as a wide receiver and halfback on the school football team. His former coach described Biden as one of the best pass receivers he'd had during his 16 years of coaching football.

Biden then attended the University of Delaware (UD) in Newark where, by his own admission, he was more interested in sports, girls, and socializing than in studying. There, he briefly played halfback for the Blue Hens freshman football team. He majored in History and Political Science, graduating with a Bachelor of Arts degree in 1965. He graduated 506th out of a class of 688. After graduation, he entered Syracuse University College of Law; he completed his law degree in 1968. Academically, he did not fare much better here than he did at UD, graduating 76th out of a class of 85.

It was during his time at the University of Delaware that Biden met his first wife Neilia Hunter. During spring break, 1964, Biden and a couple of his friends drove to Fort Lauderdale, Florida. They then decided to continue to Nassau, Bahamas. While there, the friends managed to sneak into an upscale hotel (they walked past the security guards, without incident, by wrapping hotel towels around their waists). Neilia Hunter, from New York, happened to be lying by the pool. Biden struck up a conversation with her and, by 1966, they were married.

In addition to his Bachelor of Arts and law degrees, Biden has also received honorary degrees from numerous institutions including:

- The University of Delaware.

- The University of Scranton.

- Widener University School of Law.

- Suffolk University Law School.

- Syracuse University.

- Emerson College.

Summary

Biden (as well as his siblings and parents) lived with his maternal grandparents for several years of his childhood, while the family struggled financially. Despite this, Biden has described his childhood as "stable and relatively carefree". Based on Biden's descriptions of his upbringing and his parents' roles in his life, they demonstrated strength, strong morals, and support for their son.

Overall, as a child, Biden was described as a "popular kid, if a bit quick with a punch, especially if someone teased him about his stutter". While his stutter made him a target of teasing and bullying, his determination to overcome it revealed inner strength and dogged persistence.

During his teenage years, Biden was known more for his athletic prowess than strong academic performance. Despite this, he attended the rather prestigious Archemere Academy. He then attended the University of Delaware, graduating with a Bachelor of Arts (though he finished closer to the bottom of the class than the top). He finished his formal education at Syracuse University College of Law though, admittedly, he did not finish in the top half of the graduating class.

Chapter 2: Getting His Career on Track

Overview

After obtaining his law degree, the now-married Joe Biden returned to Delaware, with his wife Neilia Hunter Biden, to work as an attorney. During the next few years, they welcomed three children: Joseph Robinette III (Beau), Robert Hunter (Hunter), and Naomi Christina (Amy).

Biden practiced law at a firm in Wilmington, while also working part-time as a public defender. In 1970, he launched his first-ever campaign for a seat on the New Castle County Council. He won the seat by over 2000 votes.

Next, Biden set his sights on becoming a senator. Neilia became his closest adviser and the 'brains' behind his campaign.

The Move into Politics

Biden served on the New Castle County Council from 1970 until 1972, when he decided to run for senate. He was considered a rank outsider and ran against the popular Republican incumbent Caleb Boggs. Biden garnered 50.2 percent of the votes in a contest fought with little resources but with a great amount of help from his family. At the young age of 29, this made Biden the fifth-youngest senator in U.S. history.

During the Vietnam War, Joe received five student draft deferments. Upon finishing his schooling, in 1968, he was reclassified by the Selective Service System as being unavailable for service as a result of having had asthma when he was younger.

Some notable moments in Biden's career, before serving as vice president of the U.S. from 2009-2017:

Biden was first elected to the Senate in 1972; he was re-elected six times.

- He served as an adjunct professor (1991–2008) at the Widener University School of Law (Wilmington, Delaware branch).

- In 1984, he led the fight to block Alabama U.S. Attorney Jeff Sessions from becoming a federal judge, due to allegations of racism.

- Biden chaired the U.S. Senate Committee on the Judiciary between the years 1987-1995.

- Biden earned both praise and criticism during his time in the Senate for his work in areas like judicial appointments, criminal justice, and foreign affairs.

- He chaired the Senate Foreign Relations Committee from 2001-2003 and, again, from 2007-2009.

- He was a former chairman, and long-serving member, of the Foreign Relations Committee.

- He played a key role in passing the (somewhat controversial) 1994 Violent Crime Control and Law Enforcement Act which hardened federal prison sentences.

- He co-sponsored the Violence Against Women Act in 1994.

- He chaired the Judiciary Committee during the then-controversial U.S. Supreme Court nomination of Robert Bork in 1987, successfully opposing Bork's nomination. Bork had been viewed as an ultra-conservative and it was feared by the Democrats that he would turn back all the more progressive advances made in the court during the preceding years. In the end, Borke's nomination was rejected by the Senate with a vote of 85-42 against, the biggest margin of any failed Supreme Court nominee.

- Biden also was a member of the International Narcotics Control Caucus. He led the charge to establish the position that oversees drug-control policy, i.e. the so-called office of "drug czar".

- His viewpoints on abortion have flip-flopped over the years. In 1974 he stated that he opposed the *Roe v. Wade* ruling and in 1981 voted for some constitutional amendments that would let certain states overturn *Roe v. Wade*. He has however changed his viewpoint since then.

- He was one of the 90 Senators who voted in favor of the Gramm–Leach–Bliley Act of 1999. The act repealed the Glass–Steagall legislation that separated investment banking and commercial banking. This allowed the combined operations to make risky investment decisions with depositors' money, which ultimately led to the 2008 crash.

- As far as his viewpoints on America's involvement in wars abroad are concerned, he has generally taken a conservative point of view. He opposed the Gulf War in 1991 but supported U.S. and NATO intervention in the war in Bosnia in 1994 and 1995. He voted in favor of authorizing the Iraq War in 2002 but opposed the increase of U.S. troops in 2007.

- He had always been against troop increases in Afghanistan, and in April 2021 announced that all American troops would be withdrawn from Afghanistan by September 11, 2021, on the 20th anniversary of 9/11.

As Senator, Biden had two unsuccessful runs towards becoming president - one in 1987 and the other in 2008. He withdrew in 1987 when it was revealed that he had plagiarized, as part of his speech, elements of a speech by, amongst others, British Labour Party leader Neil Kinnock. He withdrew from the presidential race in 2008 when he came fifth in the Iowa caucus, before joining Barack Obama's campaign as the vice-presidential nominee in 2008.

Obstacles to Overcome

If you watched the inauguration of Joe Biden—a man who had reached the pinnacle of his career and was surrounded by a devoted wife and loving, supportive family—you would, likely, not guess the amount of tragedy and pain that have made him the man he is today. Joe Biden's path to the top was not an easy one.

Car Accident

In December of 1972, mere weeks before Biden was sworn in as the senator for Delaware, tragedy struck.

In the early afternoon of December 18th, Neilia and the Bidens' three young children headed out, in the family station wagon, to run some Christmas-related errands; Biden was at work in Washington, hiring staff members. As the family vehicle pulled past a stop sign, it went directly into the path of a tractor-trailer. In Biden's own words, "My wife was killed, and my daughter was killed ... And my two boys, but for the jaws of life, and a rescue crew saving their life, would not have been around either". It was later determined that the driver of the tractor-trailer was not at fault.

His two sons, Beau and Hunter, were badly injured; Beau had a broken leg and Hunter suffered a skull fracture. Both boys eventually recovered but both spent weeks in the hospital. Biden's swearing-in, as senator of Delaware, was held in his son's hospital room.

Biden was deeply affected by this incident and, later, revealed that he had contemplated suicide, citing the fact that he could not abandon his two boys as the only reason why he did not go through with it. Biden focused on his two young boys and their well-being; that provided a reason to keep going. Indeed, while they were hospitalized, Biden visited them every day, commuting from Delaware to Washington by train. He continued to do this, daily, for the next 30 years. He became such a popular figure on the train that the Delaware station was eventually named after him!

The Campaign That Wasn't

In June of 1987, Biden first announced his run for the presidency. At 44 years of age, Biden had been a member of the Senate for over a decade and was considered a strong candidate.

In September of 1987, reports surfaced that Biden had, without proper acknowledgment, 'borrowed' portions of a speech by a UK politician, Neil Kinnock. In fact, spliced video of Biden and Kinnock surfaced and left no doubt that Biden had, indeed, used parts of Kinnock's speech.

The situation worsened. A few days later, it was discovered that Biden had used some of Bobby Kennedy's lines without proper attribution. Next came reports that, during law school, Biden had plagiarized a law review journal for a paper. Biden admitted to the incident—and to failing to cite his sources properly—but claimed that "his 1965 'mistake' was neither intentional nor malevolent".

Despite Biden's efforts to downplay the situation, the damage to his campaign was irreparable. By the end of September, he had withdrawn from the race.

Health Scare

In early 1988, Biden was working to re-establish his tarnished reputation. He was having frequent headaches (and taking Tylenol regularly) and experiencing neck pain.

In February, he delivered a speech at a university, then retired for the night. In his words, "he recalls a 'lightning flashing inside my head, a powerful electrical surge—and then a rip of pain like I'd never felt before". Biden spent the next five hours unconscious.

The following morning, he returned home and, before long, was rushed to a local hospital in Wilmington. The results of a spinal tap suggested that an artery in his brain was leaking. His best chance of survival was surgery; the chances of him surviving were 50%.

Biden survived the surgery, and, in May, a second surgery was performed—successfully. Initially, his right eyelid drooped, and the right side of his forehead was immobile. Eventually, though, the muscles began working again. By August, Biden's doctors had cleared him to return to work.

In 2019, Biden's former brain surgeon stated that Biden had not suffered any brain damage from the aneurysms or the surgeries. In fact, the surgeon indicated that he planned to vote for Biden!

2007 Campaign

In January of 2007, Biden once again announced that he would be entering the presidential race. With two additional decades of experience since his previous, short-lived presidential campaign, combined with considerable experience in the area of national security, Biden appeared to be in a better position this time around.

He drew criticism early in the campaign when, in reference to Barack Obama, he said, "I mean, you got the first mainstream African-American who is articulate and bright and clean and a nice-looking guy. I mean, that's a storybook, man". Many interpreted Biden's comments as racist but he insisted they had been taken out of context.

Despite his apparent qualifications, Biden didn't gain momentum in the polls. In January of 2008, after finishing fifth in the Iowa caucuses, he opted to withdraw from the race. Eight months later, Barack Obama announced that Biden would be his running mate as he sought the office of president.

The Passing of Beau

Beau joined the military in 2003 and rose to the rank of Major in the U.S. Army JAG Corps. In the fall of 2008, he was deployed to Iraq; he did return to the U.S. temporarily in early 2009 to attend the inauguration and his father's swearing-in as vice president. For his service in Iraq, he was awarded the Bronze Star medal.

Beau served as Delaware's attorney-general from 2006 till 2014. By all accounts, he was a rising star who was bound to follow in his father's footsteps as a senator.

In 2010, Biden's eldest son, Beau, experienced a mild stroke. Three years later, he was admitted to the hospital after feeling unwell. A small lesion on his brain was detected and removed. Initially, his condition was reported to have improved following the surgery, combined with chemotherapy and radiation. However, in 2015, Beau's symptoms worsened significantly over the period of just a few weeks. Beau died at the young age of 46.

As an interesting aside, Kamala Harris has said that she got to know Joe Biden through Beau. Harris and Beau worked closely when Harris was California's AG from 2011-2017.

The loss of Beau affects Biden to this day. At the Democratic Party Convention in August 2020, he declared "Beau is with me every single day. If he was here tonight, he would remind me 'just be who you are.' I'm a better person because of him".

Hunter's Addictions

If Beau Biden was the exemplary son, Hunter was anything but. Hunter had his first drink at the age of eight when, at a family event, he consumed a glass of champagne. By the time he was in college, he was experimenting with cocaine. At just 18 years old, he was charged with cocaine possession. However, after completing pretrial intervention and probation, the arrest was removed from his record.

As an adult, he was discharged from the Navy Reserves in 2014 after testing positive for the use of cocaine. Hunter who, at the time, was married with three daughters, issued a statement saying: "It was the honor of my life to serve in the U.S. Navy, and I deeply regret and am embarrassed that my actions led to my administrative discharge. I respect the Navy's decision. With the love and support of my family, I'm moving forward".

Hunter and his first wife, Kathleen, ended their marriage in 2016. In the divorce papers, she cited that he had spent huge sums of money on drugs, prostitutes, and gifts for girlfriends.

After the end of Hunter's and Kathleen's marriage, for a time, Hunter dated Hallie Biden, the widow of his deceased brother. While many questioned the wisdom of the relationship, the Biden family was publicly supportive and maintained that the two had bonded over the shared grief of losing Beau. After dating for a couple of years, the two parted ways. It was later discovered that, while dating Hallie, Hunter had fathered a child with another woman. Initially, Hunter claimed that the child was not his, but DNA testing proved otherwise.

In the spring of 2019, Hunter met Melissa Cohen, a South African filmmaker; they married just a week after meeting. They now have a young son, Beau.

One of the biggest controversies surrounding Hunter involves his job as a board member of Burisma Holdings, Ukraine's largest gas-production company; he joined the board in 2014. He reportedly earned a salary of $50,000 per month. Hunter's relationship with the company, and whether he had been hired due to his father's political connections, was criticized in the media during the 2020 presidential campaign. The Trump camp ruthlessly exploited the situation, citing it as an example of nepotism, and a conflict of interests. Trump's suggestions that Ukraine had meddled in the American elections or that Burisma and/or Ukraine had appointed Hunter to gain some political influence in Washington remain unproven.

Inappropriate Conduct?

In 2019, Tara Reade—a former Senate aide—accused Biden of sexually assaulting her in 1993. Biden has denied any wrongdoing in the matter.

In addition to Ms. Reade, seven other women have accused Biden of invading their personal space or touching them inappropriately. However, in these cases, the women stated that the behavior did not constitute sexual harassment or assault.

Biden's response to the accusations was somewhat unusual. He released a video that appeared to have been taken at home. In it, he acknowledged that personal space boundaries are changing; he promised to "be more mindful and respectful of people's personal space".

While there have been rumors about Biden's 'hands-on' interactions with women, thus far, none of the allegations have been proven.

Fitness For Office

Throughout the presidential campaign and during his time as a senator, Joe Biden's gaffes, mispronunciations, slurred words, and misidentification of people (once referring to his wife as his sister!) have been a source of fodder. In March of 2021, he fell three times while climbing up the stairs to board Air Force One. This came just a few months after suffering a hairline fracture in his foot, ostensibly while playing with his dog, Major.

This has raised questions as to the President's fitness to hold office, both physically and mentally. In addition to having a history of brain aneurysms, Biden has required several sinus surgeries, gallbladder removal, and the removal of some non-melanoma skin cancers.

Largely due to his age (at 78, Biden is the oldest individual to hold the position of U.S. president), combined with his medical history, some have questioned whether Biden is physically and mentally equipped to deal with the demands of his position.

In a medical summary released in 2019, Biden's primary care physician acknowledged that Biden is being treated for an irregular heart rhythm, elevated cholesterol levels, seasonal allergies, and gastroesophageal reflux. Dr. Kevin O'Connor, who has been Biden's primary care physician since 2009, stated that Biden is a "healthy, vigorous … male, who is fit to successfully execute the duties of the Presidency". The report also revealed that Biden is a non-smoker and non-drinker who exercises five days per week.

Another Chance at Happiness

Biden met his second wife, Dr. Jill Biden, Ed.D., in 1975 when he was introduced to her by his brother on a blind date. They married in 1977 at the United Nations Chapel in New York City. Like his first wife, she was (and still is) an educator.

Jill Tracy Jacobs Biden was born on June 3, 1951, in Hammonton, New Jersey, the oldest of five daughters. She graduated in 1966 from Upper Moreland High School, after which she attended the University of Delaware where she graduated with a bachelor's degree in English in 1975. She completed her first master's degree in 1981 (she has a Master of Education and a Master of Arts in English) and received her doctorate in 2007.

She continued to work at Northern Virginia Community College, throughout her term as the vice president's wife. She has indicated that she will continue teaching as the wife of the president.

Jill Biden is an accomplished author in her own right, having written three books that went on to be best sellers - *Don't Forget, God Bless Our Troops* (2012), *Where the Light Enters: Building a Family, Discovering Myself* (2019), and *JOEY: The Story of Joe Biden* (2020).

Joe and Jill have one biological child together. Their daughter, Ashley, was born in 1981. Despite having different mothers, Jill formed close connections with both Beau and Hunter.

Joe proposed five times before Jill agreed to marry him. Because the boys had already lost their biological mother, she wanted to be 100% confident in the love and relationship that she and Joe shared. During a 2019 interview, Jill revealed that it was Beau and Hunter who first brought up the idea of the couple marrying; it happened one morning, as their father was shaving. Six-year-old Hunter told his father that, "'Beau thinks we should get married.' With their father understandably confused by this pronouncement, seven-year-old Beau explained, 'We think we should marry Jill'".

Summary

Joe Biden's life, before becoming president, was one filled with highs and lows. He found love at a young age, but it was not to last. One day, he was a husband and father of three preparing to join the Senate; the next day, he was a widow and had lost, not only his wife, but his beloved only daughter. While he maintained a solid work ethic, he also prioritized his surviving children, Beau, and Hunter.

While the life paths and trials of Biden's sons were very different, as a father, he has shown tremendous love and commitment to each of them. While he was unable to save Beau from his medical issues, he has worked tirelessly to save Hunter from the cycle of addiction that could easily have been fatal.

His support of his sons has been matched by that of his wife, Dr. Jill Biden. She has shown an impressive level of devotion, not only to her husband but to the three children they raised and to her career calling as an educator.

Chapter 3: Biden's Time as Vice President

Overview

On August 23, 2008, Barack Obama officially announced Joe Biden as his running mate; on August 27, they secured the Democratic Party's nomination. On November 4, the Obama-Biden team defeated John McCain and his running mate, Sarah Palin.

Joe Biden took office as vice president on January 20, 2009. In 2012, they were re-elected for their second term, having beaten Republicans Mitt Romney and Paul Ryan.

So began the next chapter in Biden's life. For both of Barack Obama's presidencies, Biden would act as a policy expert, confidante, and friend to the most powerful man in the world.

Why Biden?

It would appear that Biden, with his experience, was expected to be a sounding board for Obama. While, initially, this may have been the case, the relationship grew into a deep friendship. While the position of vice president may have appeared, at times, to be more of a symbolic role than one that adds value, this was not the case with Biden.

Biden's vast experience as a public servant helped the administration of Obama both at home and abroad. It was on the Foreign Policy front where Biden arguably made the biggest impression during his time as vice president. Upon taking office he had been in the Senate for 36 years already, including four years as Chair of the Foreign Relations Committee. This was an important wealth of experience which Obama put to good use.

Carving his Niche

In early January 2008, then President-elect Obama delegated Biden to travel to Iraq and Afghanistan to evaluate the situation in both countries. Six months later, Biden got the job of managing the American military withdrawal from Iraq. Up to that point, Biden had been vociferous about how the war had been handled.

It was his handling of the war in Afghanistan that allowed Biden to come into his own. Indirectly tasked by Obama to act as devil's advocate on matters related to policy and defense; he frustrated the military to no end—making clear his opinions on how they were handling the war, and his issues with the surge of troops into that country. Despite his warnings to Obama to resist the military ganging up on him to get their way, this is what eventually happened, much to his frustration.

Despite these issues, Biden claimed later that Obama did not micromanage him; once he gave him instruction on foreign policy issues, he left him to his own devices. This is an indication of the level of trust that Obama had. Biden's foreign policy approach was molded much along the lines of Dick Cheney before him. His foreign policy approach was encapsulated in his motto that "all foreign policy is a logical extension of personal relationships". He successfully forged good relationships with many of his counterparts and country leaders abroad.

During his time as vice president, Biden was responsible for implementing the American Recovery and Reinvestment Act which was aimed at helping to rebuild the economy sustainably. He focused on the affordability of college studies and promoted American manufacturing growth.

He helped secure approval for the New START reduction treaty with Russia and also managed to secure new funding to maintain the U.S. nuclear laboratories. He supported the Administration's effort to re-establish leadership in the Asia Pacific. In his time as vice president, he represented America in virtually every region of the world, working to ensure the defense of Israel, liaising with Europe to ensure that an effective missile defense system would be in place, and working with South American leaders to combat drug trafficking and crime. He also built relationships with important leaders in Africa.

Some of his other achievements worthy of note:

- Pushed lesbian, gay, bisexual, transgender, queer (LGBTQ) issues to the forefront.

- Championed women's rights, especially across campuses.

- Following the death of Beau, he advocated for greater research into cancer.

- Formed a strong and lasting relationship with the President.

Joe and Barack - A Symbiotic Relationship

His eight years in the Obama White House—where he frequently appeared at the president's side—allowed Biden to share in Obama's legacy, including the passing of the Affordable Care Act, as well as the reforms and stimulus package enacted as a result of the financial crisis.

In January of 2017, in a surprise ceremony, Barack Obama presented Biden with the Presidential Medal of Freedom with Distinction after calling the vice president his 'brother' and a 'lion of American history'. This honor had only been bestowed three times before.

History is replete with examples where American presidents felt that they had to select the person who 'came second' for the presidential nomination, or someone who would toe the party line. In this case, Obama chose Biden, mainly, as a result of his sound foreign policy experience.

The relationship developed into a strong friendship that was visible for all the world to see. This extended to the relationship between their wives. Joe exclaimed on more than one occasion that it was not a case of him and Barack Obama liking each other, but a real case of brotherly love. They often ate lunch together; they even regularly exercised together and practiced their putting together on the White House putting green.

Considering this, it is surprising that Obama on numerous occasions has tried to dissuade Biden from running for president. In 2016 it was because Barack favored Hillary Clinton. Reportedly, Obama also tried to talk him out of the race in 2020; the reasoning behind his stance is unclear but it has been reported that Obama was concerned about how Biden as president might affect his own legacy.

Be that as it may, toward the end of the presidential campaign in 2020, Obama came out swinging in support of Biden. Upon confirmation of his victory, he gave a rousing celebratory speech, flaying Trump in the process. It is likely that, in the months and years to come, Biden will consult Obama for sage advice in a role reversal of their previous relationship.

Summary

The Biden/Obama partnership was an extraordinary one, characterized by mutual respect and friendship. They did not always see eye to eye on matters, but appear to have smoothed out their differences calmly and rationally.

It seems Obama deliberately selected Biden as his running mate to add experience to the administrative team. It turned out to have been a shrewd move that paid off handsomely for both men.

Their friendship continues to this day with a different dynamic. Biden does not want to appear to be relying too heavily on his former boss; Obama gives Joe the space to make his own decisions

Chapter 4: How Biden Became President

Overview

By June 6, 2020, it was evident that Joe Biden had secured enough votes to become the Democratic Party's presidential nominee. To win the nomination, a candidate has to secure at least 1,991 out of the 3,979 available pledges. At that stage, Biden had already amassed 2,000 of the pledges.

The race for the Democratic Party nominee had started in earnest in February. Biden, Warren, Bloomberg, Buttigieg, Sanders, and Klobuchar were all in the race. Biden's efforts did not get off to a good start, finishing fourth in the Iowa caucus (also his Achilles Heel in 1988) and fifth in the New Hampshire primary. He improved in the Nevada caucus, coming second to Bernie Sanders.

South Carolina was where his campaign started to turn around; he came first by a significant margin. At this stage, Buttigieg and Klobuchar dropped out of the race. Biden's next big victory came on Super Tuesday on March 3, 2020, which led to the end of Warren's campaign, followed by Sanders' campaign. He was helped when Sanders eventually gave him his full support as the

Democratic Party nominee. Until then, it had been pretty much a neck-to-neck race between the two candidates.

Road to the Nomination

Biden's road to the nomination was formally concluded at the Democratic Party Convention on August 20, 2020, when he accepted the nomination by his party. He had fought his campaign on the back of some very specific issues:

- **Health** - Biden favored an expansion of the Affordable Care Act (which he had helped Obama pass). He did not support Medicare for All but was in favor of some form of Medicare-like public option that Americans could buy into. He emphasized several times that he was not in favor of getting rid of Obamacare.

- **Taxes** - He pledged not to go aggressively after the super-rich in his taxes; the approach he promoted was to find the $1.6 trillion in so-called tax loopholes.

- **Climate change** - Biden is big on climate control. He endorsed a Green New Deal and unveiled a $1.7 trillion plan to get to zero greenhouse gas emissions by 2050. This involves inter alia, rejoining the Paris Accord, reinforcing the Clean Air Act to combat growing transportation sector emissions, and insisting that Congress pass legislation creating an enforcement mechanism to meet emissions targets, among other goals. He proposed that limiting greenhouse gas emissions should start with federal buildings.

- **Education** - Biden proposed increasing spending on schools that serve low-income students from $16 billion to $48 billion. He also wanted to improve teacher pay, expand school access for three- and four-year-olds, and invest in school mental health services. He stated that he was in favor of efforts to 'diversify' public schools. In 2015, he made a plea for free education at the College level for four years, although he has not repeated that stance during the 2020 run.

- **Foreign policy** - Biden was vehemently against Trump's 'America First' approach and stated, on numerous occasions, that he wants the U.S. to reconnect with the international community.

- **Rural America** - Biden is a strong advocate for improving the plight of rural Americans, including investing in things like rural broadband, infrastructure, clean energy, and rural healthcare.

- **Gun control** - He is a firm supporter of tighter gun control measures, including restricting the number of firearms that a person may possess, as well as limiting the acquisition of assault rifles and large magazines.

- **Immigration** - Biden stated that he was open to relaxing the limit of refugees that may enter the states and was also part of Obama's initiative of championing for the 'Dreamers,' undocumented migrants who had entered the U.S. when they were young. Oddly, as a Senator, he voted in favor of the Secure Fence Act which made provision for extending the border wall.

- **Abolishing the Electoral College** - He did not support this.

- **Criminal justice reform** - He revealed ambitious plans for reforming the criminal justice system, including abolishing the death penalty, building private prisons, mandatory minimum sentences for non-violent crimes, and the general reduction of prison sentences by focusing on other options for rehabilitation.

- **Reproductive rights** - As mentioned earlier, he has changed his viewpoints on this from being staunchly in line with his Catholic beliefs in the eighties to a recent statement saying that he does support abortion. In early 2021, he reiterated that all reproductive rights should be available to all women.

- **Reparations** - Again, this is an issue on which he seems to have changed his mind. In the seventies and eighties, he was violently against any form of reparations but, more recently, has suggested there could be exceptions. Thus, it is difficult to know what his true viewpoint is on the matter.

There were some noteworthy facets of his acceptance speech as the Democratic nominee on August 20, 2020. He delivered an outstanding speech, arguably the best of his career. Not widely known for strong oratory skills, this was one time he pulled it off successfully. The announcement of Kamala Harris as his vice-presidential candidate also broke new ground, as she was the first female vice-presidential candidate. It also seemed as if the Democrats had overcome, at least for the time being, their internal differences and squabbles. Biden strongly emphasized his bipartisan approach to running the country and reached out to all voters to unite in the interests of the country. Only time will tell whether that will be the case.

The Presidential Debates

After securing his party's nomination, and before having the election, in time-honored American tradition, it was time for the two parties' candidates to participate in debates. While COVID-19 played havoc with the 2020 debate schedule, two occurred.

The first debate took place on September 29 and, in true Red v. Blue tradition, it was no holds barred. It was a messy affair in which the two candidates constantly interrupted one another. Topics covered included the GOP Supreme Court nomination of Judge Amy Coney Barrett (which, eventually, successfully pushed through), the Affordable Care Act, handling of the coronavirus pandemic, navigating the economy through the pandemic, tax cuts, the radical left and right, the upcoming elections, and the possibility of electoral fraud.

Neither participant had much reason to hold their head high afterward. The debate ended in name-calling, with the moderator having lost control of proceedings.

The second and final debate took place on October 22. This time the participants' microphones were muted when the other spoke so there could be no interruptions. At play were topics like climate control, with Biden taking a distinctive visionary approach with his emphasis on renewables while Trump reinforced the importance of the oil economy. Other topics covered included their various foreign policy viewpoints on the Middle East and China, as well as possible foreign interference in the election.

According to a CNN poll, 53% of viewers believed that Biden had won the debate, while 39% considered Trump the winner. Overall, the debate did little to significantly move impressions about either candidate, as also shown by the poll.

In the United States, election day is always the first Tuesday following the first Monday in November (in this case, November 3, 2020). Even though the election took place during the COVID-19 pandemic, voter turnout was the highest since 1900, and more votes were cast than in any previous U.S. presidential election.

Biden was declared the winner by the Associated Press and major media outlets on November 7. His win was confirmed in the Electoral College on December 14. On January 6, 2021, Congress certified his victory. President Trump launched more than 50 legal challenges, refusing to concede defeat. He insisted that there was voter fraud, but no supporting evidence of fraud has been found.

On Wednesday, January 20, 2021, Joseph R. Biden Jr. was sworn in as the 46th U.S. president. At the same ceremony, Kamala D. Harris was sworn in as the first female, the first Black American, and the first person of South Asian descent to be elected vice president.

Summary

Americans have grown accustomed to presidential races being tough, animated, and even spiteful at times. The 2020 race set a new high (or, perhaps one should say, a new low) in this regard. After having beaten tough competitors from within the Democratic stable, Biden eventually got the better of Trump in the second of two debates; both of the debates were ugly affairs.

Despite having a strong Republican showing at the polls, Biden won. Some would argue his victory was due to articulating his policy choices better than Trump had, particularly his views on health, immigration, and foreign policy.

Chapter 5: Biden's Biggest Successes

Overview

The jury is still out as to how Biden's presidency will be rated. His past successes, or lack thereof, are well documented and we touched upon those in the previous chapters. We will highlight some of those again. As for his term in office, at the time of writing this book, it is too early in his presidency to make an astute assessment.

Apart from that, he seems to be treated more cordially by the press than his predecessor was, making it a difficult task to assess how effective he has been thus far. One significant advantage he had going into the presidency was the fact that he previously served as vice president for eight years. This will no doubt give him a significant headstart compared to most previous presidents.

When one wants to know how effective an individual is in, virtually, any aspect of life, it is wise to examine what 'enemies' are saying. In this regard, we will look at the Russian, Chinese, and Iranian reactions to Biden's presidency since he took office.

As Senator and Vice President

First, let's take a look at his successes in his earlier life as Senator.

The fact that he was elected senator at age 29, then re-elected six times, before running for vice president says something about his popular appeal to the folks of Delaware.

Biden is known as a very capable dealmaker and has a management and deal-striking style that takes an inclusive approach towards reaching compromise. This is supported by his friendly and coercive leadership style which makes him imminently likable.

Joe Biden is someone who seems to learn from his mistakes and has, on numerous occasions, admitted making a bad decision and even publicly apologized. Examples of this include when he was accused of less than appropriate behavior towards women (he tends to touch them when he speaks to them), as well as when he conducted the Clarence Thomas SCOTUS nomination (1991), where he was taken to task for his Committee's treatment of Anita Hill. He apologized to her years later.

Biden sponsored or cosponsored 4,445 pieces of legislation. Of these, 396 passed both Houses and 348 became law.

Between 1987 and 1995 he served on the Senate Foreign Relations Committee. He also spent 17 years on the Judiciary

Committee, including periods as chair and ranking minority member. These are important assignments only given to those who are deemed to have the proper background and ability.

Some other achievements include:

- In 1979, he assisted with securing the Strategic Arms Reduction Treaty (START) between the U.S. and the Soviet Union, reducing the risk of a global nuclear conflagration.

- In 1984, introduced the Violence Against Women Act.

- In 1986, he introduced the Senate Climate Bill. This also led to the establishment of a task force on global warming.

- In 1993, he oversaw the process of introducing Ruth Bader Ginsburg as the second woman in the history of the Supreme Court.

- In 1994, was one of the main proponents of the Police Officers' Bill of Rights.

- In 1994, he co-authored the Crime Bill.

- In the 1990s, he supported U.S. intervention in the Yugoslav Wars which resulted in putting a stop to ethnic cleansing and facilitated bringing peace to that part of the world.

- In 2001, he was part of the team that wrote anti-terror legislation which culminated in the adoption of the Patriot Act.

- In 2001, he—together with Mitch McConnel—introduced a bill for across-the-board budget cuts.

- In 2006, he co-sponsored the Palestinian Anti-terrorism Act which makes provision for the 2-state solution.

- In 2008, he promoted U.S. participation in UN climate activities and has throughout encouraged increased support for renewable energy. He has utilized his considerable experience to establish bipartisan plans to cut carbon emissions and promote a sustainable future.

- In 2008, he introduced the Criminal History Background Checks Pilot Extension Act which allows volunteer organizations to obtain criminal history background checks on their volunteers.

- In 2008, he was the sponsor of the Protect Our Children Act, which assists law enforcement agencies to prosecute child predators.

- In 2009, he oversaw the allocation of $90 billion for clean energy as part of the 2009 Recovery Act.

- In 2009, he oversaw the execution of the American Recovery and Reinvestment Act which was, until that stage, the largest economic recovery plan in U.S. history.

- In 2010, he helped pass the Affordable Care Act, known then as Obamacare.

- In 2014, he brokered bipartisan negotiations in the Senate to pass the Budget Control Act.

- Also in 2014, he led a review of federal employment and training programs.

- In 2016, he helped to launch the Cancer Moonshot initiative to assist with the diagnosis and treatment of cancer.

- Biden supports the 2nd Amendment but has on numerous occasions expressed his disdain for the ease with which people can get access to firearms, especially assault rifles.

- He has established close ties with many foreign leaders and their representatives through, among other avenues, the Foreign Relations Committee.

- During his time as a senator, he supported the expansion of NATO by including Poland, Hungary, and the Czech Republic.

Views of Other Countries

As we said at the beginning of this chapter, it is important to view Biden's appointment from the viewpoint of his most important opponents abroad.

China was one of the last countries to congratulate Biden on his win. Clearly, China is somewhat cautious about Biden. Trump imposed unilateral tariffs on the country and triggered a trade war which was to the detriment of both countries and, indeed, the global economy. Biden, with his significant foreign policy experience, is expected to use existing multinational platforms like the WHO, G-20, World Bank, etc. to hold China accountable.

The GOP has been quick to exploit Biden's previous statements regarding China. For example, in April 2021, the GOP Political Action Committee (PAC) launched an ad campaign showing Biden and China's president, Xi Jinping, together. One of the ads featured Biden saying China is "not bad, folks" followed by an image of Biden and Xi; the images were from Biden's time as vice president when then-president Barack Obama sent Biden to Japan to meet with Xi.

In another ad, related to a speech Biden gave in 2011, he stated that "a rising China is a positive development". It is to be doubted whether China's present policy approach towards the U.S. will be influenced by those statements of Biden, which were made some time ago.

Russia could not have hoped for a better relationship than with Trump who had been strangely enamored by Putin. Biden's approach to relations with that country does not appear to follow Trump's precedent; sanctions were imposed on Russia in April 2021.

When learning that Biden was coming to power, Iran announced that it was raising its oil output, probably in expectation of a lowering of sanctions by the new administration. Biden has expressed a willingness to go back to the negotiation table on Iran's nuclear enrichment program. However, the Middle East remains a volatile environment where Biden's fortitude will be tested over the next few years.

Summary

In March 2021, 73% of Americans approved of the way he was handling the pandemic, and 60% approved of the way he was handling the economy.

He has been instrumental in launching many policy instruments and bills in U.S. history, as well as overseeing numerous committees and programs. His legacy in this regard is a significant portfolio of bills, acts, and other policy instruments.

These are some of Biden's biggest successes. One could justifiably ask, what about failures?

Chapter 6: The Biggest Criticisms Against Biden

Overview

Joe Biden has also made his share of mistakes. However, one should judge his 'mistakes,' which we will get to shortly, in the context of a few considerations:

- The fact that American society has evolved. What may have been socially and politically acceptable four decades ago may not be so anymore. Race relations and matters related to LBGT rights are cases in point. The same may be said about law enforcement and the public's perception about how to engage with the police.

- A person evolves as a human being and tends to grow more mature in thinking and reasoning skills. Biden was young when he first became a senator and has, no doubt, learned much during his years in the Senate and, particularly, during his years as vice president.

- The American value system has changed a great deal over the past 40 years. Not only in relation to the points mentioned but also regarding perceptions on foreign policy, the environment, and society in general. So, although some of the issues that we will discuss are listed as 'mistakes,' they could also be considered 'changes in perspective.'

Criticisms

Let us, therefore, consider these, perhaps for a lack of a better word, 'inconsistencies' about Joe Biden:

- The Crime Bill (1994), regarded by some as one of his successes, has been criticized for the fact that it led to unjust mandatory minimum sentences and other harsh provisions, impacting black men in particular. In 2016, Biden defended his crime bill saying, "I'm not ashamed of [the Crime bill] at all. As a matter of fact, I drafted the bill. We talk about this in terms mostly of 'black lives matter.' Black lives really do matter, but the problem is institutional racism in America. That's the overarching problem that still exists". In the run-up to the elections and in the face of the multiple police shootings of Black men over the past two years, this has been one of the main points on which he was attacked – both by members of his own party and by the opposition.

- In line with the previous point – he sponsored several bills related to the war on drugs (which is also seen as one of his successes by his constituents). His critics claim that these bills addressed the symptoms of the drug problem, not the causes, and that it resulted in significant unequal treatment and incarceration of minorities.

- In 1996, Biden was one of 32 Senate Democrats who voted for the Defense of Marriage Act which, essentially, prevented same-sex marriage. As previously mentioned, since then he has expressed differing opinions on the matter; he opposed attempts to introduce a Constitutional amendment that would allow states to ban same-sex marriage. In 2012, however, he expressed himself in favor of same-sex marriage even before President Obama did (some would argue that he embarrassed the president in the process). He has taken other steps since then to advance gay and transgender rights.

- In 1994, Anita Hill testified about how she was sexually harassed by Justice Clarence Thomas. Hill claimed that she was forced to defend herself against powerful men when Biden should have sought to have independent witnesses, who could have added credence to Hill's claims. Biden has since apologized and admitted that he could have done more to support her.

- During law school at Syracuse, Biden was guilty of plagiarizing. He admitted to this but was permitted to continue with his studies. Years later, plagiarism once again became an issue when he copied portions of speeches by John F. Kennedy, Hubert H. Humphrey, and Neil Kinnock. Biden also, falsely, boasted of having finished in the top half of his class at law school. He later admitted that these claims were inaccurate.

- He voted against welfare in the 1990s in support of Bill Clinton. The subsequent program of welfare 'reform' is generally considered to have failed.

- Voted to turn around the Glass-Steagall act. This was one of the measures put in place after the Great Depression to create a division between investment banking and FDIC-guaranteed deposits. This prevented banks from gambling with depositors' money. Biden later said it was one of his worst mistakes.

- He opposed the integration of schools in the 1970s. Liberal leaders wanted to pursue more aggressive integration policies but when they saw the backlash from white voters, they apparently changed their minds. Here, he also changed his viewpoint from being in favor of integration during the seventies, where he made statements to the effect that he favored school desegregation but was not in favor of putting in place policies where all races had to use the same buses.

- Biden voted for the Iraq War although he stated that he was against it. At the time, he was chair of the Senate Foreign Relations Committee which raises some eyebrows as to why he did not do more to advise President Bush to a contrary cause of action.

- It is generally recognized that Biden's strength is his foreign policy experience. But after leaving the Obama Cabinet, former Defense Secretary Robert Gates said of Biden in his memoirs, "Joe Biden was wrong on nearly every major foreign policy and national security issue over the past four decades".

Summary

As should be obvious from much of the above, deciding whether many of Biden's actions in the past were successes or failures is a matter of much conjecture and depends on which side of the political aisle one sits. Washington is, after all, hardly a place where political parties applaud each other's achievements.

Closely related to the issues of successes and failures is the matter of Biden's political viewpoints and the related objectives that he has pursued, or for that matter, is still pursuing.

Chapter 7: Biden's Primary Political Stances and Objectives

Overview

Joe Biden is a politician and, to a point, must bow to the whims of his party. The fact that he has changed his views on several issues over the years is in line with political rhetoric and, as mentioned before, viewpoints tend to change over time as society evolves.

Here we delve into several issues that have been prominent during his first few months in office. Note that these may change or be refined during the rest of his tenure, but are accurate at the time of writing this book.

The First Few Months

The first 79 days of his presidency were characterized by a slew of executive orders, laws, and policy proposals. These suggest he is keen to get the job done as rapidly as possible – much to the surprise of both his party and the GOP.

Many Democrats had feared that his approach to decision-making, characterized in the past by an approach of gradual change rather than rapid action, would stand in the way of speedy decisions. Also, because of his outspoken preference for bipartisan decision-making, there was concern that he would want to involve the Republicans in just about everything. They were wrong.

From the GOP's point of view, they were surprised because of their traditional viewpoint of him as 'Slow Joe.' Despite Biden's strong belief in arriving at bipartisan solutions, he watched President Barack Obama fail to reach an agreement with the GOP on many matters. This instilled in him a belief that the spirit and nature of the 'old' GOP had gone which is why he now seems to be making his own unilateral decisions on policy matters.

So, how did he do?

COVID-19

The biggest challenge facing Biden when he took office was, of course, to address the coronavirus. His initial response included launching a national contact-tracing program, establishing a scheme for free testing for all, and hiring 100,000 people to set up the tracing program.

The aim was to establish a minimum of 10 testing centers in every state. He called on national agencies to deploy resources in support of this initiative. Time will tell whether some of his other directives, such as stating that all governors should mandate wearing masks, will stand the test of time.

Other details surrounding his approach to COVID-19 include:

- Getting rid of economic hurdles. This includes making sure no citizen has to assume the cost of COVID testing or treatment. This includes amending the Public Health Service Act and the Social Security Act, as well as expanding the National Disaster Medical System.

- Getting the world together in a joint effort to confront this crisis and future ones. To this end, he has called for an international cooperative effort to combat pandemics, including the establishment of a Global Health Emergency Board.

- Restoring trust in and credibility of the government. The aim here is to rebuild the public's trust in government and the national health system by, amongst others, restoring the White House National Security Council Directorate for Global Health Security and Biodefense.

- Creating an effective national emergency response against COVID-19. There are many initiatives here, but one of the most important is to task all health authorities to ensure that hospital capacity will be optimized to handle any potential future surges in the number of patients.

- Putting economic measures in place to help families and small businesses to survive. This includes setting up a Health Crisis Unemployment Initiative and ensuring that unemployment insurance benefits will be available to those who lose their jobs as a result of COVID

The Economy

The total of Biden's economic stimulus bill amounts to $1.9 trillion which is bigger than any measure of similar nature in U.S. history.

Biden has an overarching economic policy called the 'Build Back Better' plan. Listed below are some of the key components of this plan:

The plan, in particular, addresses the needs of two categories of citizens – young people and blue-collar workers. These are also the people that helped him get to power. He unveiled a $2 trillion infrastructure plan in February.

Among his proposals to assist families and small businesses is an additional $200 in monthly Social Security payments, canceling

Trump-era tax cuts, and providing $10,000 of student loan forgiveness for federal loans. He is also in support of increasing the federal minimum pay to $15 an hour.

Another initiative is a $2tn investment in green energy and a $400bn commitment to buy American goods. This is in parallel with the bigger undertaking to introduce 'Buy American' laws for any transport projects to be implemented. This is clearly in response to critics who had previously lamented the fact that Biden had supported the North American Free Trade Agreement (NAFTA), in the process effectively moving jobs overseas. In further support of this, his 2021 undertaking is for the government to invest $300bn in U.S.-origin goods and services, including technology and research.

Criminal Justice Reform

Although he has rejected calls to defund the police, he has moved away from his tough stance on criminal justice which characterized his tenure as a senator in the 1990s. As a result of the 2020 race riots, he has stated that he believes that racism is endemic in U.S. society and that it needs to be addressed aggressively. In support of this, he has proposed the creation of a business support fund of $30bn.

He now proposes policies to reduce prison sentences, address inequality in gender, race, and income within the justice system, and rehabilitate prisoners who have been set free. He would also now create a $20bn program to motivate states to invest in incarceration reduction efforts, eliminate minimum prison sentences, decriminalize marijuana, and clear the criminal records of people who were previously convicted on cannabis possession, and end the death penalty.

According to Biden some money for police should be redirected to social service programs like mental health. He has furthermore called for a $300m investment in a program that will promote community policing.

In a controversial move, he has set up a commission to investigate the composition of the Supreme Court from 9 to 13 justices with the opposition claiming that he wants to "pack the court". This is also a policy matter on which Biden has had a change of mind over the years. In 1983, as a junior senator, he called the idea of court-packing a "boneheaded idea". He has had significant pressure from the progressive left within his party and that pressure, as well as the Republicans' push-through of a replacement for the late Ruth Bader Ginsburg close to the 2020 election, have influenced his thinking on the matter. If a change in the number is made it will not be the first time in American history. Since the Supreme Court was established by the

Judiciary Act of 1789 it has varied in numbers from as low as five to as many as 10 justices.

Climate Change

In late January, Biden proposed an extensive plan to reduce the U.S.'s dependence on fossil fuels. This has not been well received, especially by GOP supporters of the oil economy. He has since had America rejoin the Paris Climate Accord which Donald Trump withdrew from.

He has also, much to the chagrin of the GOP, canceled the Keystone XL pipeline project.

Although he is not a supporter of the Green New Deal as forwarded by the left-wing of his party, he did propose a $1.7tn federal investment in green technologies research over the next 10 years. There is still a focus on the U.S. to reach net-zero emissions by 2050. On 22 April 2021 Biden committed the U.S. to reduce its greenhouse gas emissions by 50%-52% below the 2005 emission levels by 2030. These goals, albeit part of the Paris Accord, are non-binding. At the time of writing this book, the administration has not provided a plan as to how these targets will be met. Popular opinion is that this will be done through a combination of greater forestation, reduced emissions by factories, much more focus on electric vehicle development, as well as a dramatic increase in subsidies for renewables. This is also expected to create many more blue-collar jobs.

On 23 April 2021 Biden stated that he is planning to engage in partnerships with countries like India, Sweden, United Arab Emirates, and the United Kingdom to "decarbonize critical sectors across the board".

Since taking office Biden had the U.S. also rejoin the World Health Organization and the Paris Accord.

Make America Great Again?

As previously stated, Biden's strength lies in his ability to engage with foreign leaders. During his campaign, he emphasized that his priority would be national issues. Despite this, it is clear that Biden will move away from Trump's isolationist policies and is ready to engage with the rest of the world again. In this regard, he wants to renew ties with former U.S. allies and, in particular, with NATO.

He is also strong on curbing China's emergence on the world stage as a key player. He has indicated that China should, indeed, be held accountable for unjust trade and environmental issues. However, he has proposed international cooperation with other countries, as opposed to tariffs. Exactly how that would be implemented and what it would look like remains to be seen.

Health Insurance

It is estimated that Biden's proposed public health insurance scheme would cost $2.25tn over 10 years. The aim is to insure about 97% of Americans. Although he stopped short of the universal health insurance proposal of some of his more progressive party members, his undertaking is to give all Americans the option to enroll in a public health insurance option similar to Medicare. He also wants to lower the eligibility age for Medicare itself from 65 to 60 years.

Border Control

In February, Biden revealed an extensive immigration plan which his predecessor called a reversal of everything 'achieved' in the previous four years. On February 2, 2021, the White House released the *Fact Sheet: President Biden Outlines Steps to Reform Our Immigration System by Keeping Families Together, Addressing the Root Causes of Irregular Migration, and Streamlining the Legal Immigration System.* It stated that the executive actions would:

- Create a task force whose focus would be reuniting families that were separated at the border during Trump's presidency.

- Develop a strategy to establish a humane asylum system and address irregular migration across the southern border. This involves a "three part-plan for safe, lawful and orderly migration in the region." Biden also promised that Central American refugees and asylum seekers could enter the U.S. using legal methods.

- Restore Americans' faith in the legal immigration system and promote the successful integration of immigrants who enter the U.S. with hopes of opportunity and freedom.

By March 2021, it had become clear that, next to the COVID-19 issue, this had become the biggest test of Biden's young presidency. More and more people were piling up on the southern border and his deputy who had been tasked to resolve the issue had by then not even visited the border. Republicans were screaming blue murder, pointing to all the 'good' things done by Trump that were now being undone, while there is a strong push from the more liberal elements within the

Democratic Party to completely decriminalize illegal border crossings.

Education

With the money gained from reversing some of Trump's tax cuts, Biden has proposed or supported proposals on policy issues related to student loan debt forgiveness, expansion of tuition-free colleges, and universal preschool access.

Other specific initiatives include the following:

- Ensuring that the $60 billion allocated for education in the COVID-19 relief package is rapidly distributed to districts and institutions of higher education.

- Addressing the digital divide, so that low-income students and students of color have better and more rapid access to learning materials and classes.

- Doubling the number of psychologists, counselors, nurses, and social workers in schools to assist especially those students who are battling with the trauma of the COVID-19 pandemic.

- Reinstating the Obama-era guidance on school discipline. This will benefit especially LGBTQ students and students of color.

- Doubling the Pell Grant to help low-income students afford college.

Gun Control

Biden has urged for more action on curbing the ease with which Americans can purchase arms, especially assault rifles. He also wants to enforce extensive background checks for firearm licenses.

In early April 2021, he announced half-dozen executive initiatives to combat gun violence in America. These initiatives, although important, do not contain any legislative actions with real 'bite.' To do that with an evenly divided Senate will require new legislation to get 60 votes to pass which seems like an impossibility considering that would mean adding 10 Republican votes for any such initiative—if all the Democrats support such a bill.

The measures that he did announce include the following:

- Seek to limit the "ghost guns"—firearms that are homemade and lack serial numbers—as well as make it easier for individuals to identify family members who should be prohibited from buying firearms.

- An attempt to toughen up regulations on pistol-stabilizing braces.

- The introduction of two bills that require background checks on all purchases and transfers of firearms and allow a 10-day review period for gun purchases.

- Government is working on proposed rules for changing the definition of a firearm to include lower receivers, which is an essential part of a semiautomatic rifle.

Biden, although already having done more to cut down on the proliferation of firearms than most of his predecessors, has already found out that there is a huge gap between ambition and execution when it comes to firearms control in the U.S. The mighty National Rifle Association, although much weakened as a result of financial and other problems, still carry significant clout in the Capitol.

Summary

Biden has pushed through a raft of executive orders, laws, and policy proposals. Time will tell whether he can stick with the pace, both physically and mentally.

The important thing that stands out at this stage is the extent to which his undertakings on the campaign trail are aligning with what he is doing in practice. This bodes well for the rest of his tenure as president, although he is likely to come up against some significant challenges. At home, the COVID pandemic and the economy are likely to be his two major challenges, although there are other significant issues to deal with, including healing the divide between right and left. On the foreign policy front, he is likely to be significantly challenged by developments within China, Russia, and Iran. Considering his background and experience, these issues may be easier for him to deal with than the ones at home.

So, if these are then Biden's political viewpoints and objectives, how do they intertwine with what is expected from him during his tenure as 46th president?

Chapter 8: What is in Joe Biden's Future?

Overview

Regardless of whether Biden serves for one or two terms, his approach to the job and on main policy issues is likely to remain the same. Despite him changing his mind over the years on matters like same-sex marriage, packing the court, policing, and incarceration, most of his central-leftist policy stances remain intact. Though the vagaries of international actors on the world stage may force him to abandon some deeply held beliefs on how to conduct foreign affairs.

As far as Joe Biden's future is concerned, we may, therefore, analyze this on two levels: a personal one and one as President of the United States.

On a Personal Level

On a personal level, there has been much speculation about whether Biden, as a 78-year-old when taking office, will have the mental and physical fortitude to see through even one term, not to mention two. There are numerous examples of gaffes that he has made over the years during his public speaking, and during the run-up to the presidential election, a number of those were apparent again, making some question whether the President may not be already suffering from some sort of mental impairment, like perhaps the early stages of dementia. The two brain surgeries that he had in 1988 did not do much to quell suspicions in this regard although doctors did pronounce him mentally fit after the operations.

It has also raised questions about his appointment of Kamala Harris and whether this was not a deliberate ploy by the Democratic Party to pave the way for the first black women to become president, should Biden have to step down due to health issues. This is a prospect that should make both sides of the aisle nervous, as Harris' first three months in office have not exactly been encouraging, especially as far as her handling of the border crisis is concerned. She has notably kept a low profile in general.

The Policy Route

On a policy level, we have touched on some of his viewpoints and objectives in the previous chapter. We take a look at some of the likely developments over at least the short term of this tenure as president:

- **Rebuilding alliances** - Having already started on this path, it is clear that Biden wants to restore relationships internally as well as abroad. The divide and vitriol that has characterized the U.S. over the past four years have left indelible scars on the American social and political landscape. As the generally recognized 'nice' guy, Biden is likely to reach out to all to try and mend American society, although his trust in the GOP may have been shaken as a result of their perceived attitude of non-cooperation the last four years. He has however all but admitted that there is no other choice. Internationally he has made his ambitions clear. The trick of course here is to follow up and whether Biden, at his age, will have the physical strength to pursue the very ambitious agenda that he has set for himself and his administration.

- **The China issue** - Although Biden has said that the policy towards China needs to be a collective one in which also Europe should take part, the real litmus test of his new suggested rules-based approach towards China will lie in the impact that it will have on his Asia-Pacific allies, especially Taiwan and Japan. For them, the odds are much higher of having a China triggered by an uneven and sloppy approach towards foreign policy. One of the most stringent tests may come from China's recent reaffirmations about its ambitions of unifying China and Taiwan, as it had always said it would.

- **Regaining the trust of NATO** - Working with Brussels to establish the levels of trust seen in decades gone by may take some time. Even if the relationship should be repaired, it is doubted whether it will be on the same level as before. A large part of the American populace has grave doubts about the nature and scope of the transatlantic relationship and whether it is worth the time and money, especially when there are so many internal issues to be addressed.

- **The economy** - In the previous chapter, we did discuss the Biden viewpoints and actions thus far on the economy. Having policy viewpoints and spending plans is one thing, however. Implementing them successfully is quite another. Time will tell, but Biden's plan to raise taxes on corporate profits and American households making upwards from $400,000 per year is likely to be significantly resisted by the GOP.

- **Ties with Africa** - Trump did significant harm to African relationships with some racialized pronouncement about the continent. It will take some time for Biden to restore the faith of African leaders in the administration. He is however likely to keep a deep

American interest, even physically so, in developments in Somalia, the Sahel, and the new emerging ISIS ties in Mozambique. Some new policy tools on the horizon could aid him in this regard. These include the $500-750 million Africa Trade and Investment Program (ATIP) and the equity-backed U.S. International Development Finance Corporation (DFC).

- Relationship with the Middle East - The Middle East has always been a hotbed of activity, militarily and politically so, and the U.S. involvement in Iraq and Afghanistan has severely impacted the level of trust that many countries in the region had for America. Some specific challenges will be in the relationships with Israel, Saudi Arabia, Iran, and Turkey. Although Biden is not expected to rock the boat in the short term, there may very well be some longer-term readjustments to come. There will likely be a move towards a more nuanced view of the Israel-Palestine question. In Turkey, Erdogan's flirtations with Russia and problems caused by him in the Mediterranean with gas exploration, setting the stage for potential clashes with Israel and/or Greece, are issues that are likely to come up for greater scrutiny. To further compound matters, on April 23, 2021, Biden informed Erdogan that he was going to recognize the 1915 massacre of Armenians by the Ottoman Empire as a genocide. This is in line with Biden's approach which has become apparent since he has taken over of informing world leaders of statements that he is going to make to the press beforehand, if he knows that it will irritate them. But the biggest challenge in the region is likely to come from an erratic Iran, who in April 2021 declared that it has increased its uranium enrichment process to 60% levels - far more than needed for peaceful purposes. Biden has since taken part in trying to re-establish the Joint Comprehensive Plan of Action (JCPOA), accepted by Iran in 2015 but subsequently canceled by Trump.

- **Relationship with Latin America** - Biden is expected to follow a balanced approach, more so in any case than his predecessor, to address issues related to human rights abuses, poverty, and migration. The latter will feature highly on his agenda, as he has been an expressed supporter of engaging in dialogue with South and Central American countries to stop the tide of refugees coming to the southern border from these countries. So, instead of building a wall around the U.S., literally and figuratively so, Biden is all for addressing the root causes of the migration problem at the source.

- **The U.S. and Europe** - Biden will welcome the emergence of a stronger, more united Europe. This will be an aid on multiple fronts, not least of which is Iran and China. Although the EU may seem to have been weakened with the departure of Britain, this is likely to be a short-term issue.

Summary

Joe Biden will be 82 years old in 2024. Will he run for a second term? It is to be doubted. But much of what will be his legacy will develop over the next four years. His challenges are many. His work ethic is to be admired. Apart from having to deal with old adversaries like China and Russia, his other great challenge will be to restore America's status in the world as a true superpower who may be admired and trusted. To achieve that within four short years, may be a bridge too far.

Conclusion

Joe Biden is a human being just like you and me. He is likely to make mistakes and has shown that he is also capable of great achievements. From a humble and poor beginning, he developed into becoming the most powerful person on the planet. Yes, there were lows. We covered his traumas, his gaffes, his alleged flirtations with women, and his plagiarism mistakes. But let us look in more detail at what we covered in this book.

In Chapter 1 we looked at his place of birth, his parents, growing up, and his schooling. We showed that whilst being a good sportsman and strong leader, he did not excel academically and at college was regularly in the last third of his class. But hard work and a strong sense of self-pride instilled in him by his parents ensured that he overcame hurdles like his stuttering through sheer willpower and effort, leaving him ready to take on the world when he graduated from law school in 1968. This was also the year during which he married his first wife, Neilia.

In Chapter 2 we looked at Joe's early career, including his life as a U.S. Senator. We covered a list of the most important things that he achieved during his time. We also looked at his traumatic experiences, including the loss of his first wife and their daughter in a car accident less than a month after he was elected as a senator for the first time, the loss of his son Beau in 2015, Hunter's exploits, his health issues, and the matter of allegations that he has had to face over the years of inappropriate behavior towards women. We also discussed his marriage to his second wife, Jill, and provide a brief overview of her background. It is clear that she has a significant influence in his life and that much of his policy stance on education is influenced by her and especially by her viewpoints on community colleges.

In Chapter 3 we looked at Biden's time as vice president, how he had gotten there, and the relationship between him and Barrack Obama. We also covered some of his achievements during that period, pointing out that it was especially in the foreign policy side that Biden tended to excel. Biden and Obama developed a close personal relationship, more so than most other running mates in the history of the U.S. Strangely enough, Obama did not seem to be too keen on Biden following him as president, preferring Hillary Clinton for the role in 2016, and also attempting to dissuade him from running in 2020.

In Chapter 4 we covered how Biden became president. His run-up to being nominated by the Democratic Party as their nominee in August 2020, having seen off several strong contenders in the process. We covered the presidential debates and then the election itself which saw Biden being sworn in as the 46th president of the U.S. on 20 January 2021. The competition within the Democratic Party was a fierce one, as was the run-up to the election with Trump.

In Chapter 5 we looked at Joe Biden's biggest successes. The list is long and is testimony to a lifelong career of service as a professional civil servant. We also covered the viewpoints of China, Russia, and Iran in this regard. It is still too early within his presidency to know how relations with those three countries will turn out but based on early pronunciations it would seem as if the relationship with Russia and China may be heading for a cold spell, whereas the relationship with Iran is presently being tested by that country's renewed uranium enrichment efforts, as well as by the new negotiations around the JCPOA.

In Chapter 6 we covered some of the criticisms against Biden. Although there are many, it important to note that many of these originate from the other side of the aisle who are not normally given to flattery of a sitting Democratic president. And of course, vice versa. Also, that whilst Biden may have erred in his younger career, hindsight is 20/20, and with the passage and wisdom of time, by his own admission, he may have plotted a different course on some matters.

In Chapter 7 we discussed Biden's primary political stances and objectives. We covered a whole raft of topics, from COVID-19 to policing and gun control. Joe Biden may be described as a center-leftist within the Democratic Party, meaning that he will have a progressive agenda that will have to consider also the wishes of the radical left within his party. At the same time, his Catholic background is likely to deter him from making too many drastic concessions to those elements within his party. He has to walk a very narrow and difficult path to appease people within his party, not to mention the GOP. We also indicated that while in his term as a senator he was very much for bipartisan solutions to the country's problems, his tenure under Obama may have shown him that it is fruitless to attempt this. Only time will tell if that will become an entrenched point of view.

In Chapter 8 we looked at the future of Joe Biden, both from a personal and political point of view. On a personal level, considering his age there remains doubt in many quarters as to whether Biden will be able to see out even his first term, not to mention a second. By the end of his first term, he will be 82. He was already the oldest president-elect in history. Counting in his favor is the fact that he has a fit and healthy lifestyle. Professionally, we looked at a number of his policy viewpoints as they are likely to emerge over the next months and years. This is made difficult by the fact that he has been on the job for only a few months at the time of writing, but at the same time, he has shown great fortitude and a high work ethic pushing through several bills, executive orders, and policy proposals.

Joe Biden—the man, father, husband, and 46th President of the United States of America. Seldom in history has a man had to take over the leadership of the country under such perilous and trying circumstances. At the beginning of this book, we said that one of the reasons for writing this book is to determine whether we have a man that is up for the job in these difficult times through which America, and indeed the world, is going.

Did we answer that? We leave it to the reader to decide, but one thing is certain - the host of national and international challenges that Biden is facing will put him to the test!

References

Agiesta, J. (2020, October 23). *CNN Poll: Biden wins the final presidential debate.* CNN. https://edition.cnn.com/2020/10/22/politics/cnn-poll-final-presidential-debate/index.html

All About Joe Biden. (n.d.). Google. https://sites.google.com/site/infojoebiden/home/childhood

Amaro, S. (2020, November 27). *China is more concerned by Biden than Trump, economist Jim O'Neill says.* CNBC. https://www.cnbc.com/2020/11/27/why-biden-is-more-concerning-for-china-than-trump.html

Archmere Academy (n.d.). *Archemere Academy: About us.* https://www.archmereacademy.com/welcome/about-us#:~:text=Archmere%20Academy%20is%20a%20private,developing%20students%20into%20empathetic%20leaders.

Biden, J., Dr. (April 26, 2019). *Why I was initially reluctant to marry Joe Biden.* Time. https://time.com/longform/jill-biden-joe-biden-marriage-proposal/

Biography.com Editors. (May 3, 2021). *Joe Biden biography.* A & E Television Networks. https://www.biography.com/us-president/joe-biden

Breuninger, K., & Wilkie, C. (2020, September 30). *Vicious first debate between Trump and Biden offered little on policy, lots of conflict.* CNBC. https://www.cnbc.com/2020/09/29/first-presidential-debate-highlights-trump-vs-biden-.html

Broder. J. (October 23, 2008). *Father's tough life an inspiration for Biden.* The New York Times. https://www.nytimes.com/2008/10/24/us/politics/24biden.html

Brownstein, R. (January 19, 2021). *Trump leaves America at its most divided since the civil war.* Cable News Network. https://www.cnn.com/2021/01/19/politics/trump-divided-america-civil-war/index.html

Bueno, A. (January 20, 2021). *Inside Joe Biden's history of heartbreaking tragedy and triumph.* Entertainment Tonight. https://www.etonline.com/inside-joe-bidens-history-of-heartbreaking-tragedy-and-triumph-151904

Caldera, C. (September 16, 2020). *Fact check: Biden, like Trump, received multiple draft deferments from Vietnam.* https://www.usatoday.com/story/news/factcheck/2020/09/16/fact-check-biden-received-multiple-draft-deferments-vietnam/5809482002/

Chan, M. (January 12, 2017). *Read the full transcript of President Obama surprising Joe Biden with the Medal of Freedom.* Time. https://time.com/4633826/joe-biden-obama-presidential-medal-freedom/

Cillizza, C. (2021, April 9). *The sneaky radicalism of Joe Biden's first few months in office.* CNN. https://edition.cnn.com/2021/04/09/politics/joe-biden-environment-guns-filibuster/index.html

Cockburn, A. (2019). *No Joe! Joe Biden's disastrous legislative legacy.* Harper's Magazine. https://harpers.org/archive/2019/03/joe-biden-record/

Cranley, E., Pasley, J., & Frias, L. (2020, October 1). *Meet Hunter Biden, the often scandal-plagued middle child of Democratic presidential nominee Joe Biden.* Insider. https://www.businessinsider.com/hunter-biden-life-scandals-ukraine-involvement-with-trump-giuliani-2019-9?IR=T

Crump, J. (2021, January 20). *What happened to Joe Biden's father? President references his dad's unemployment in inaugural address.* Independent. https://www.independent.co.uk/news/world/americas/us-election-2020/joe-biden-dad-father-inauguration-speech-b1790296.html

Darby, L. (2019, August 18). *Obama repeatedly tried to get Biden not to run for President.* GQ. https://www.gq.com/story/obama-to-biden-dont-run

Dickenson, J. (1987, September 22). *Biden academic claims "inaccurate."* The Washington Post. https://www.washingtonpost.com/archive/politics/1987/09/22/biden-academic-claims-inaccurate/932eaeed-9071-47a1-aeac-c94a51b668e1/

Dr. Jill Biden FIRST LADY. (2021). The White House. https://www.whitehouse.gov/administration/dr-jill-biden/

Egan, L. & Pettypiece, S. (April 8, 2021). *Biden targets 'ghost guns' and 'red tag' laws in new gun control measures.* NBC News. https://www.nbcnews.com/politics/white-house/biden-target-ghost-guns-red-flag-laws-new-gun-control-n1263438

Enten, H. (2021, March 27). *Why Biden has an immigration policy problem.* CNN. https://edition.cnn.com/2021/03/27/politics/biden-immigration-border-analysis/index.html

Fregni, J. (2021, January 22). *The future of education under the Biden administration.* The Future of Education. https://www.teachforamerica.org/stories/the-future-of-education-under-the-biden-administration

Glueck, K. (2020, September 22). *7 takeaways from the Democratic National Convention*. The New York Times. https://www.nytimes.com/2020/08/21/us/politics/dnc -takeaways-biden-obama.html

Godfrey. (n.d.). *15 things to expect from Joe Biden's presidency and promises to Americans.* Atlantic Ride. https://www.atlanticride.com/what-exactly-are-joe-bidens/

Hendrickson, J. (n.d.). *What Joe Biden can't bring himself to say.* The Atlantic. https://www.theatlantic.com/magazine/archive/2020/0 1/joe-biden-stutter-profile/602401/

Holzberg, M. (2021, April 15). *From 'bonehead idea' to studying it: Joe Biden's shifting positions on court packing.* Forbes. https://www.forbes.com/sites/melissaholzberg/2021/0 4/15/from-bonehead-idea-to-studying-it-joe-bidens- shifting-positions-on-court-packing/?sh=5ad8c53b63ea

Hook, J. (2019, March 18). *The burden of a 40-year career: Some of Joe Biden's record doesn't age well.* Los Angeles Times. https://www.latimes.com/politics/la-na-pol- biden-senate-record-controversies-20190318-story.html

Igoe, K. (October 21, 2020). *Who was Joseph R. Biden Sr., Joe Biden's father?* Marie Claire.

https://www.marieclaire.com/politics/a33573986/who-was-joseph-r-biden-sr/

Jaffe, A., Madhani, A., & Balsamo, M. (2021, April 9). *Biden orders gun control actions — but they show his limits.* The Associated Press. https://apnews.com/article/joe-biden-violence-merrick-garland-gun-politics-gun-violence-7ddb30681ca3abbf1a0faa286e3df7b2

Joe Biden. (n.d.). Ballotpedia. https://ballotpedia.org/Joe_Biden

Joe Biden. (2021, January 21). Biography Newsletter. https://www.biography.com/us-president/joe-biden

Joe Biden 46th president of the United States. (n.d.). National Geographic. https://kids.nationalgeographic.com/history/article/joe-biden

Joe Biden, date of birth, place of birth. (n.d.). Born Glorious. https://www.bornglorious.com/person/?pi=6279

Joe Biden just won the presidency: What does that mean for America's role in the world? (2020, November 7). Atlantic Council. https://www.atlanticcouncil.org/blogs/new-atlanticist/joe-biden-just-won-the-presidency-what-does-that-mean-for-americas-role-in-the-world/#ElectionBidenEurope

Joe Biden President of the United States. (2021, March 31). Brittanica. https://www.britannica.com/biography/Joe-Biden

Joe Biden profile: Third White House run lucky for "Middle Class Joe." (2021, January 20). BBC. https://www.bbc.com/news/world-us-canada-51682000

Joe Biden sworn in as 46th U.S. president. (n.d.). U.S. Embassy in Costa Rica. https://cr.usembassy.gov/joe-biden-sworn-in-as-46th-u-s-president/

Joe Biden: Where does he stand on key issues? (2021, January 19). BBC. https://www.bbc.com/news/election-us-2020-53575474

Joe Biden's lasting legacy as Vice President. (n.d.). HuffPost. https://www.huffpost.com/entry/joe-bidens-lasting-legacy-as-vice-president_n_587fc3e8e4b0d9f0a9a2fe05

Joe's story. (n.d.). Democratic National Commitee. https://joebiden.com/joes-story/

Kalter, L. (2020, October 28). *A closer look at Joe Biden's health.* Web MD. https://www.webmd.com/a-to-zguides/news/20201028/a-closer-look-at-joe-bidens-health

Kim, L. (2021, January 6). *Beau Biden, the late son of Joe Biden, is still a strong presence in his father's life.* Town & Country. https://www.townandcountrymag.com/society/politics/a33638261/who-was-beau-biden-joe-biden-son/

Liptak, K. (2021, April 23). *President Biden told Turkish President Erdoğan he's planning to recognize Armenian genocide.* CNN. https://edition.cnn.com/2021/04/23/politics/biden-erdogan-armenian-genocide/index.html

List of Joe Biden's accomplishments. (2020, November 4). Miami-Dade Democratic Party. https://www.miamidadedems.org/joe-biden-accomplishments-list

March, L. (August 20, 2020). *A look back at Joe Biden's days as an athlete.* The Daily Pennsylvanian. https://www.thedp.com/article/2020/08/joe-biden-penn-athletics-football-archmere-2020-election-delaware

Melton, M. (2017, January 14). *VP Biden leaves legacy of hard work, deep friendship, internet humor.* VOA. https://www.voanews.com/usa/us-politics/vp-biden-leaves-legacy-hard-work-deep-friendship-internet-humor

Miller, K. (2021, March 24). *Who is Joe Biden's wife, Dr. Jill Biden? 13 things to know about the potential First Lady.* Women's Health. https://www.womenshealthmag.com/relationships/a32 171112/joe-biden-wife-jill/

Minayo, P. (2020, November 7). *Joe Biden biography, background, education, career and family.* Who Owns Kenya. https://whownskenya.com/index.php/2020/11/07/joe-biden-biography-background-education-career-and-family/

Motevalli, G., & Shahla, A. (2020, December 7). *Iran views Biden presidency as opportunity to pump more oil.* World Oil. https://www.worldoil.com/news/2020/12/7/iran-views-biden-presidency-as-opportunity-to-pump-more-oil

Mumford, A. (2020, December 8). *The foreign policy of Joe Biden: Assessing his Vice Presidential legacy.* The Foreign Policy Centre. https://fpc.org.uk/the-foreign-policy-of-joe-biden-assessing-his-vice-presidential-legacy/

Murray, M., & Holzberg, M. (2021, April 22). *GOP super PAC releases new ads targeting Biden on China*. NBC. https://www.nbcnews.com/politics/meet-the-press/blog/meet-press-blog-latest-news-analysis-data-driving-political-discussion-n988541/ncrd1186221#blogHeader

Nagle, M. *Nearly 50 years after death of wife and daughter, empathy remains at Joe Biden's core*. https://abcnews.go.com/Politics/50-years-death-wife-daughter-empathy-remains-joe/story?id=74814251

Newman, M. (June 24, 2019). *How Joe Biden went from 'Stutterhead' to senior class president*. Delaware Online. https://www.delawareonline.com/story/news/2019/06/24/how-joe-biden-overcame-stutter-class-president-archmere-high-school/1261174001/

O'Boyle, I. (n.d.). *The Irish ancestry of Joe Biden*. Ancestor Network. https://www.ancestornetwork.ie/the-irish-ancestry-of-joe-biden/

Pramuk, J. (December 17, 2019). *Joe Biden's doctor says the 77-year-old White House hopeful is 'healthy' and 'vigorous.'* CNBC. https://www.cnbc.com/2019/12/17/joe-biden-campaign-releases-health-summary-from-doctor-in-2020-primary.html

Pruitt, S. (2018, October 28). *How Robert Bork's failed nomination led to a changed supreme court.* History. https://www.history.com/news/robert-bork-ronald-reagan-supreme-court-nominations

Raedle, J. (2021). *Presidential elections.* History. https://www.history.com/topics/us-presidents/presidential-elections-1

Relman, E., & Sheth, S. (2020, May 4). *Here are all the times Joe Biden has been accused of acting inappropriately toward women and girls.* Insider. https://www.businessinsider.com/joe-biden-allegations-women-2020-campaign-2019-6?IR=T

Sancya, P. (2020, June 6). *Biden secures Democratic presidential nomination for November showdown against Trump.* MSNBC. https://www.nbcnews.com/politics/2020-election/biden-secures-democratic-presidential-nomination-november-showdown-against-trump-n1226101

Sciutto, J., Liptak, K., & Atwood, K. (2021, April 15). *How Biden went his own way on Afghanistan withdrawal.* CNN. https://edition.cnn.com/2021/04/14/politics/biden-overrules-advisers-afghanistan-withdrawal/index.html

Solender, A. (OCtober 8, 2020). *Biden says he won't state opinion on court-packing until after election.* Forbes. https://www.forbes.com/sites/andrewsolender/2020/10/08/biden-says-he-wont-state-opinion-on-court-packing-until-after-election/?sh=6a9c10759dc4

Stanton, Z., & Muller, J. (2020, May 3). *55 things you need to know about joe biden.* Politico. https://www.politico.com/news/magazine/2020/03/05/biden-2020-president-facts-what-you-should-know-campaign-121422

Starkey, J. & McMichael, W.H. (October 16, 2014). *Failed drug test leads to discharge of Biden's son.* Delaware Online. https://www.delawareonline.com/story/news/politics/2014/10/16/failed-drug-test-leads-discharge-bidens-son/17396767/

Stiehm, J. (2016, December 5). *Bidding Biden goodbye.* U.S. News. https://www.usnews.com/opinion/thomas-jefferson-street/articles/2016-12-05/a-hard-look-at-joe-bidens-political-legacy-before-his-vice-presidency-ends

Sullivan, K., & Liptak, K. (2021, April 22). *Biden announces US will aim to cut carbon emissions by as much as 52% by 2030 at virtual climate summit.* CNN. https://edition.cnn.com/2021/04/22/politics/white-house-climate-summit/index.html

Superville, D. *Hunter Biden details lifelong addiction struggle in memoir.* ABC News. https://abcnews.go.com/Entertainment/wireStory/hunter-biden-repeat-work-ukrainian-firm-76785487

Tapper, J. *A Biden problem: Foot in mouth.* ABC News. https://abcnews.go.com/Politics/story?id=2838420&page=1

Taylor, P. (September 18, 1987). *Biden admits to plagiarizing in law school.* The Washington Post. https://www.washingtonpost.com/archive/politics/1987/09/18/biden-admits-plagiarizing-in-law-school/53047c90-c16d-4f3a-9317-a106be8f6102/

The Biden plan to combat coronavirus and prepare for future global health threats. (n.d.). Battle for the Soul of the Nation. https://joebiden.com/covid-plan/

The RS Politics 2020 Democratic Primary policy guide. (2020, March 3). Rolling Stone. https://www.rollingstone.com/politics/politics-lists/2020-democratic-candidates-issues-policy-positions-820811/

Travers, K. (January 7. 2010). *Vice president's mother, Jean Finnegan Biden, passes away at 92.* ABC News. https://abcnews.go.com/Politics/vice-president-joe-bidens-mother-jean-finnegan-dies/story?id=9506417

Travis, A. (2020, August 17). *Fact check: Did Joe Biden really have brain surgery?* Distractify. https://www.distractify.com/p/did-joe-biden-have-brain-surgery

Turley, J. (April 10, 2021). *Did Joe Biden pack the Supreme Court commission to simply fail?* The Hill. https://thehill.com/opinion/judiciary/547495-did-joe-biden-pack-the-supreme-court-commission-to-simply-fail

Vallejo, J. (2021, March 22). *Joe Biden falls three times stumbling up stairs of Air Force One.* Independent. https://www.independent.co.uk/news/world/americas/us-politics/joe-biden-fall-air-force-one-b1819731.html

Vazquez, M., & Sullivan, K. (2021, April 23). *Biden makes the economic case for fighting climate change on second day of virtual summit.* CNN. https://edition.cnn.com/2021/04/23/politics/white-house-leaders-climate-summit-day-two/index.html

Vice President Joe Biden. (n.d.). The White House. https://obamawhitehouse.archives.gov/realitycheck/node/110

Vinjamuri, L., Vakil, S., Bata, A., Sabatini, C., Benton, T., & Geall, S. (2020, October 23). *Final US Presidential debates: Five key highlights.* Chatham House.

https://www.chathamhouse.org/2020/10/final-us-presidential-debates-five-key-highlights

Washburn, L. (2020, October 17). *Joe Biden's 46-year Washington success story.* The Spectrum. https://www.thespectrum.com/story/opinion/2020/10/17/washburn-joe-bidens-46-year-washington-success-story/3695504001/

Weindling, J. (2019, April 25). *The 10 worst things Joe Biden has done in his political career.* Paste. https://www.pastemagazine.com/politics/joe-biden/the-10-worst-things-joe-biden-has-done-in-his-poli/#10-biden-voted-for-the-iraq-war

Weissert, B. (2021, April 12). *Biden Republicans? Some in GOP open to president's agenda.* The Associated Press. https://apnews.com/article/some-gop-open-to-biden-agenda-7858050374c244239578f00745ba4450

Wilkie, C. (April 4, 2019). *Biden promises in video message to be more 'mindful and respectful of people's personal space.'* CNBC. https://www.cnbc.com/2019/04/03/biden-promises-to-be-more-mindful-of-peoples-personal-space.html

Woodward, A. (December 7, 2020). *Neilia Hunter Biden: How the deaths of Joe Biden's first wife and daughter changed his politics.* Independent.

https://www.independent.co.uk/news/world/americas/
us-politics/neilia-hunter-biden-death-naomi-
b1826865.html

Yglesias, M. (2019, April 15). *Joe Biden is the Hillary Clinton of
2020.* Vox.
https://www.vox.com/2019/1/10/18173132/joe-biden-
hillary-clinton-2020